MEDIA SOURCES

INTERNET

Published by Creative Education
P.O. Box 227
Mankato, Minnesota 56002
Creative Education is an imprint of The Creative Company.

DESIGN AND PRODUCTION BY **ZENO DESIGN**

PHOTOGRAPHS BY Corbis (Latin Stock; Gabe Palmer), Getty Images
(Colorblind Images, Leland Bobbe, Micahel Brown, FREDRICK FLORIN/
AFP, Chris Hondros, Lester Lefkowitz, Jeff J. Mitchell, Mike Powell;
Steven Puetzer, Peter Sherrard, ROBERT SULLIVAN/AFP, SEIJI TAJIMA/
SEBUN PHOTO, Mario Tama)

Photographs on pages 11 and 15 courtesy of Image Science & Analysis
Laboratory, NASA Johnson Space Center

LIBRARY OF CONGRESS CATALOGING-IN-PUBLICATION DATA

Bodden, Valerie.
Internet / by Valerie Bodden.
p. cm. — (Media sources)
Includes index.
ISBN 978-1-58341-557-3
1. Internet—Juvenile literature. I. Title. II. Series.

TK5105.875.I57B623 2008
004.67'8—dc22   2006101002

First edition

9 8 7 6 5 4 3 2 1

MEDIA SOURCES

Internet

VALERIE BODDEN

CREATIVE

The Internet is used by people across the world. Most schools have Internet **access**. So do most companies. You might have Internet access at home, too!

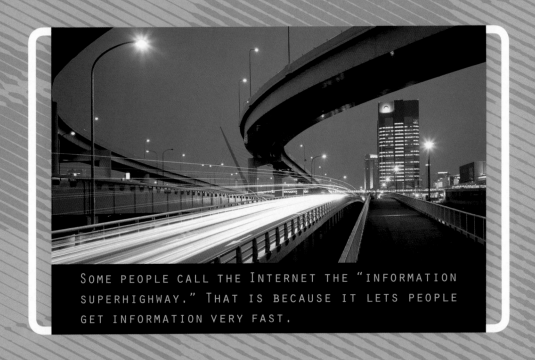

SOME PEOPLE CALL THE INTERNET THE "INFORMATION SUPERHIGHWAY." THAT IS BECAUSE IT LETS PEOPLE GET INFORMATION VERY FAST.

LOTS OF STUDENTS USE THE INTERNET

The Internet was created about 40 years ago. The Internet is a computer **network**. The network joins computers around the world together.

[7

MOST WORKPLACES USE THE INTERNET

The computers are joined by wires called cables. Some of the cables are under the ground. Some hang from poles. Messages called signals move through the cables. They move very fast! Some signals move through the air, too.

CABLES JOIN COMPUTERS TOGETHER

One part of the Internet is called the World Wide Web. The World Wide Web is where you can look at **Web sites**. There are all kinds of Web sites. Some have fun facts. Others sell things. Some have games you can play!

SOME PEOPLE LIKE TO SPEND TIME GOING FROM ONE WEB SITE TO ANOTHER. THIS IS CALLED "SURFING THE NET."

THE INTERNET GOES AROUND THE WORLD

Each Web site has an address. Most Web site addresses start with "http://www." Then they give the name of the Web site. There are no spaces in the name. The name for the San Diego Zoo Web site is "SanDiegoZoo."

YOU CAN WATCH TV SHOWS OR EVEN MOVIES ON SOME WEB SITES!

[13]

BIG ZOOS HAVE THEIR OWN WEB SITES

Some Web site addresses end with "com." Others end with "gov." Some end with "org." A full Web site address looks like this: "http://www.nasa.gov." This is the Web site of a group of people who study outer space.

SOME PEOPLE USE THE INTERNET TO DO BAD THINGS TO OTHER PEOPLE'S COMPUTERS. THESE PEOPLE ARE CALLED "HACKERS."

THE NASA WEB SITE IS ABOUT SPACE

The Internet has search engines, too. A search engine is a kind of Web site. It lets you type in what you are looking for. Then it lists lots of Web sites about that thing.

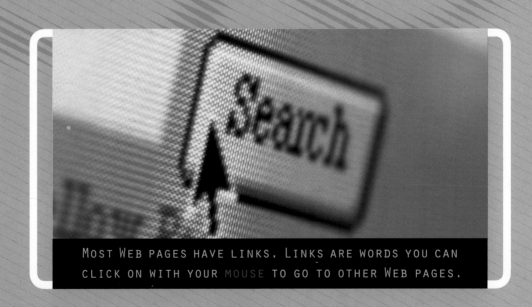

MOST WEB PAGES HAVE LINKS. LINKS ARE WORDS YOU CAN CLICK ON WITH YOUR MOUSE TO GO TO OTHER WEB PAGES.

GOOGLE IS THE NAME OF A SEARCH ENGINE

You can use the Internet to send e-mail. To send e-mail, you type your message on a computer. Then you send it using the computer. E-mail goes very fast! It can go around the world in a few seconds!

ALL E-MAIL ADDRESSES USE THE "@" SIGN. YOUR E-MAIL ADDRESS MIGHT LOOK LIKE THIS: "MYNAME@HOTMAIL.COM."

THE INTERNET IS USED IN LOTS OF PLACES

Today, people work to make the Internet better. They try to make it easier to find Web sites. They try to make Web sites that can do more things. And they try to get more and more people to use the Internet!

SOME PEOPLE CALL MAIL THAT IS SENT THROUGH THE POST OFFICE "SNAIL MAIL." THAT IS BECAUSE IT IS A LOT SLOWER THAN E-MAIL.

```
i=0;  i<=1;  i++)

cor[aInd   ] = i;
l(aIn           ector);
```

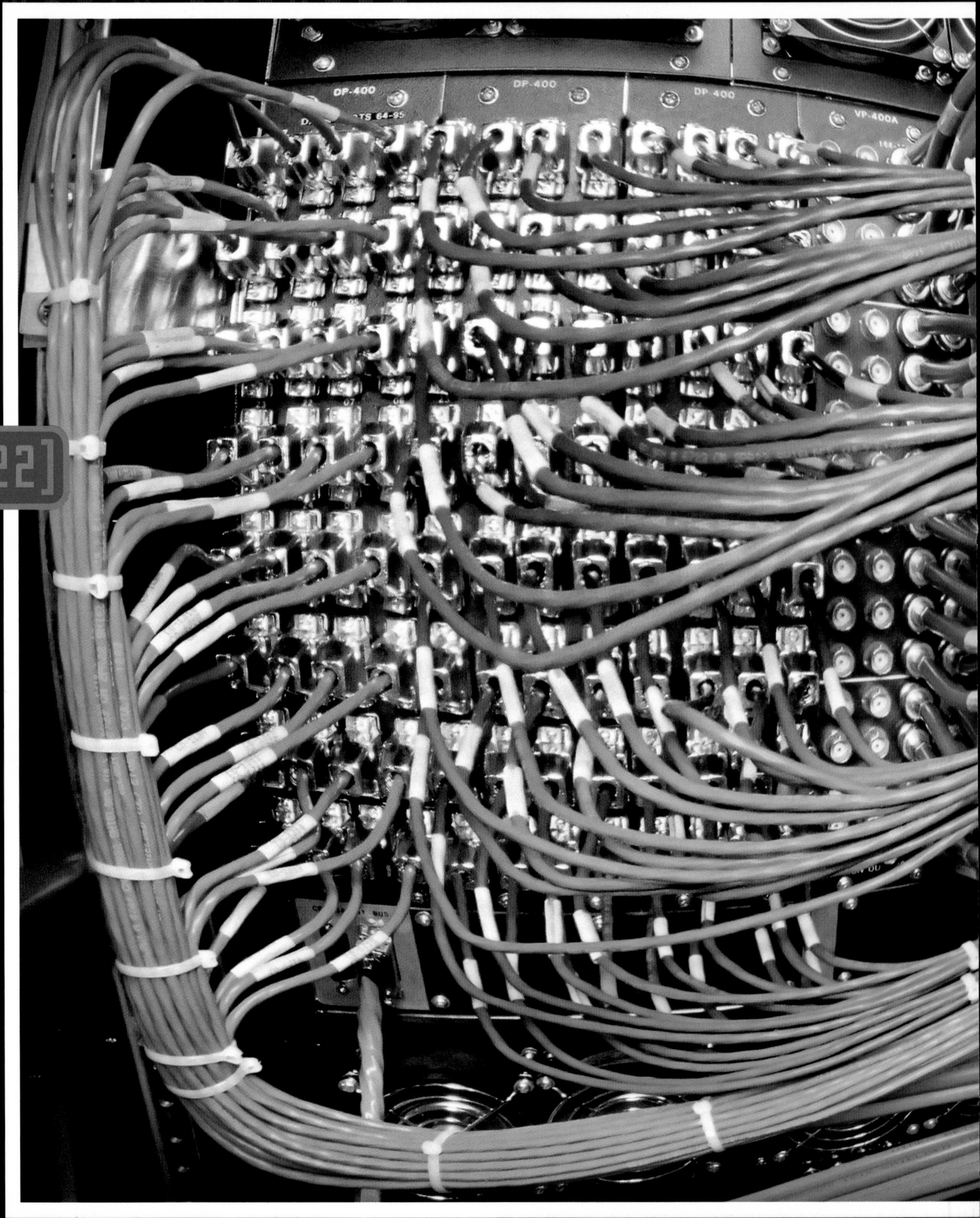
DP-400
DP-400
DP-400
VP-400A

GLOSSARY

access the ability to connect to the
Internet

mouse a part of the computer that you
slide to move the pointer across the screen

network a group of computers joined
together by cables or by signals that go
through the air

Web site a group of Web pages; Web
pages are pages that you can see by going
on the World Wide Web

INDEX

cables   8

e-mail   18, 20

Internet access   4, 23

links   16

network   6, 23

search engines   16

Web site addresses   12, 14

Web sites   10, 12, 14, 16, 20, 23

World Wide Web   10